THE MINIATURE BOOK OF
Potpourri

JUDY TAYLOR

CRESCENT BOOKS
New York

This 1991 edition published by Crescent Books, distributed by Outlet Book Company, Inc., a Random House Company, 225 Park Avenue South, New York, New York 10003, U.S.A.

© Salamander Books Ltd., 1991
129-137 York Way, London N7 9LG, United Kingdom

Printed and bound in Belgium

ISBN 0-517-03390-9
8 7 6 5 4 3 2 1

CREDITS

MANAGING EDITOR: *Jilly Glassborow*
EDITED BY: *Veronica Ross*
PHOTOGRAPHY BY: *Helen Pask*
DESIGN AND ARTWORK BY: *Pauline Bayne*
TYPESET BY: *SX Composing Ltd.*
COLOR SEPARATION BY: *P&W Graphics, Pte. Ltd.*
PRINTED IN BELGIUM BY: *Proost International Book Production, Turnhout, Belgium*

CONTENTS

INTRODUCTION   8

GOLDEN SCENT   10

DAISY DAYS   12

SWEET ROSE   14

MEADOWSWEET   16

COTTAGE GARDEN   18

RAINBOW   20

LAVENDER BLUE   22

MINTY GREEN   24

SWEET HONEYSUCKLE   26

RED ROYAL   28

ORIGINAL LAVENDER   30

SPRING MEMORY   32

FOREST WALK   34

HARVEST TIME   36

AUTUMN BREEZE   38

LAVENDER BOTTLES   40

SCENTED BAGS   42

PRETTY PARCELS   44

$\mathcal{I}$NTRODUCTION

$\mathcal{T}$he concept of perfuming a room has been with us for generations. In days gone by fresh herbs and flowers were used to mask unpleasant odours, and every large house had its own herb garden for medicinal as well as cosmetic use. Gradually the first pot-pourris were created, and many fascinating and varied recipes have been handed down over the years.

Instead of reaching for a synthetic room freshener, try making your own pot-pourri. It's fun to experiment with herbs and flowers from your own garden and you will soon build up an interesting collection of material. Leaves, grasses, nuts and seeds can be used as well as scented flowers to add interesting textures and fragrances to your pot-pourri mix.

Drying your chosen flowers is easy. Choose healthy blooms picked on a dry day. Spread the flowers onto sheets of newspaper and leave in a warm and airy place to dry; hang any herbs in bunches. After about a week they will feel papery and will be ready to use. Once you have all your dried ingredients ready the next step is to use a fixative in order to save the fragrance. The best fixative to use at home is powdered orris root which is widely available and very effective. Course salt and spices such as cloves, cinnamon and nutmeg also act as fixatives as well as adding an even greater variety of scents to the mixture. The final ingredient is essential oil which reinforces the natural perfume. Use this sparingly; most recipes will only need four or five drops. Mix well and leave in an air-tight container for six weeks.

When making your own pot-pourri, look out for variation of colour and texture and don't be afraid to experiment with different combinations of flowers and leaves, herbs and spices to create your own special, fragrant mixtures.

GOLDEN SCENT

∽

2 cups of dried rose petals and buds
1 cup of lemon verbena leaves
2 cups of mixed flowers including pansy, helichrysum
(strawflower or everlasting), yarrow and mimosa
½ cup of powdered orris root
1 chopped vanilla pod and 2 chopped cinnamon sticks
6 broken bay leaves
Shredded dried peel of one lemon
2 teaspoons of ground allspice
1 teaspoon of ground clove
Oil of cloves and oil of rosemary

The flowers for this deliciously fragrant pot-pourri have been chosen for their colour and texture as well as their scent. The addition of lemon peel adds a pleasant lemony aroma.

Using a large wooden bowl, rubbed with oil of cloves, mix all the dried flowers together. Now add the other ingredients and a few drops of essential oil of rosemary. Mix well, then seal in a jar to blend and mature for six weeks, opening the jar occasionally to stir the contents.

$\mathscr{D}$AISY DAYS

3 cups of pink carnation petals
3 cups deep pink rose petals and rose buds
2 cups white clover flower heads
1 cup camomile flowers
1 cup crimson carnation petals
1 cup of broken pink and white statice flowers
1 cup of lavender seed heads
3 teaspoons of powdered orris root
½ teaspoon of powdered cloves
2 or 3 drops of lavender oil or carnation oil

$\mathscr{D}$aisy days is a delicate pot-pourri, ideal for a bedroom with its soft shades of pink and cream and subtle fresh fragrance.

Gather all your chosen flowers, putting aside a number of whole camomile and clover flowers to scatter over the finished pot-pourri. Combine all the other dried ingredients in a large bowl and mix them together gently. Carefully add 2 or 3 drops of either the oil of lavender or the oil of carnation. Store in an airtight containers for six weeks, then decant.

$\mathcal{S}$WEET ROSE

6 cups of strong scented rose petals
6 bay leaves – finely chopped
4 vanilla pods
2 tablespoons of coarse salt
(one for sprinkling over)
1 tablespoon of ground nutmeg
1 tablespoon of dried orris root powder
1 tablespoon of powdered cinnamon

This pot-pourri is made by a slightly different method, even though it uses all dried ingredients again. The addition of vanilla pods gives the pot-pourri an exotic and unusual aroma.

You will need a large, dry screw top jar for this pot-pourri. Mix all the ingredients together well, apart from the vanilla pods. Place the vanilla pods round the edge of the jar in an upright position. Now fill the jar carefully with layers of your mixture, sprinkling the salt between each layer. Finish with a final layer of salt on top. Secure the jar tightly and leave undisturbed for a month.

MEADOWSWEET

2 cups of pink clover flowers
2 cups of pink rose petals
2 cups of lemon mint and apple mint leaves
1 cup of marjoram and meadowsweet
1 cup of thyme and sage leaves mixed
1 cup of deep pink statice flowers
1 cup of rose geranium leaves and flowerheads
1 cup of elderflowers
½ cup of bucha leaves
1 tablespoon of grated lemon peel
3 teaspoons of powdered orris root
2 or 3 drops of patchouli oil

Meadowsweet is one of the prettiest recipes and looks delightful poured into low baskets with handfuls of pink clover flowers and dried grasses strewn on top. Gather all your dried flowers and herbs. Pour them into a large mixing bowl, and blend well. Now add the lemon peel, orris root and a few drops of the patchouli oil. Stir again, and store in air tight containers for about six weeks.

COTTAGE GARDEN

2 cups of mixed rose petals
1 cup of lavender flowers
1 cup of scented geranium leaves
plus a few lemon balm leaves
1 cup of mixed sweetpeas, pink and purple
1 cup of pink rosebuds
1 cup of jasmine flowers
½ cup of honeysuckle flowers
½ cup of dianthus (pinks) petals – Mrs Sinkins
2 teaspoons of orris root powder
2 or 3 drops of rose geranium oil
½ cup of pink helichrysum flowers

Many of the lovely flowers from your garden can be used to make this deliciously fragrant mixture. Making sure your flowers and leaves are well dried, place in a large mixing bowl and stir gently. Sprinkle on the orris root powder, which is an important preservative, and stir again. Now add your essential oil very carefully a drop at a time. Pour into air tight containers and store in a dry spot for about six weeks.

RAINBOW

2 cups of red and yellow rose petals
1 cup of chopped bay and lemon balm leaves
1 cup of scented geranium leaves
2 cups of lavender flowers
1 cup of blue mallow flowers
and cornflowers
1 cup of camomile (anthemis) flowers
½ cup of marigold flowers
½ cup of powdered cloves and allspice
1 tablespoon of dried lemon peel
2 tablespoons of powdered orris root
3 or 4 drops of lemon verbena oil

This pot-pourri makes a perfect gift. The glowing shades of the blue, red and yellow flowers and the fresh lemony aroma combine to make this a special recipe.

Collect your prepared ingredients, reserving a few whole blue mallow flowers and camomile flowers to scatter on top. Mix all the dried ingredients together in a large bowl. Add the essential oil, lemon verbena, sparingly. Mix again, then store in airtight containers for six weeks.

_L_AVENDER BLUE

≈

3 cups of lavender flowers
1 cup of rosemary mixed with
cologne mint leaves
1 cup of blue delphinium flowers
1 cup of larkspur flowers
1 cup of mauve and blue statice flowers
1 tablespoon of dried lemon peel
1 teaspoon of mixed spice
3 drops of lavender oil

This mixture looks lovely in dishes with a few whole larkspur or delphinium flowers lying on top. Alternatively display in a silver bowl, to reflect the cool tones of the blue and purple hues.

After cutting bundles of fresh lavender, hang them to dry in a warm airy place, then strip the lavender flowers from the twigs. To make the pot-pourri, put all the dried ingredients into a large bowl. Mix them together well with your fingers. Add the lavender oil very carefully, one drop at a time. Mix again, then pour into airtight containers.

MINTY GREEN

1 cup of pennyroyal leaves
1 cup of crushed bay leaves
1 cup of basil and rosemary leaves
1 cup of peppermint leaves
1 cup of cologne mint leaves
1 cup of broken eucalyptus leaves
1 cup of sage and southernwood
½ cup of ground cloves
2 or 3 drops peppermint oil

For a change gather together a selection of green leaves and mixed herbs for this fresh minty pot-pourri. You can place this mixture in bowls or use it to fill little muslin bags to hang by an open window. Mix all the dried ingredients together in a large bowl. Then very carefully add the peppermint oil, one drop at a time. Too much can ruin the delicate balance of your pot-pourri mixture, and you want to aim for a fragrance that is subtle but not overpowering. Stir the ingredients well making sure the oil is absorbed. Pour into airtight containers and store in a warm dry place for six weeks.

SWEET HONEYSUCKLE

∾

3 cups of dried marigold flowers
2 cups of honeysuckle
2 cups of gold and yellow rose petals
1 cup of mimosa flowers
1 cup of orange and gold carnation petals
1 cup of golden rod flowers
1 cup of yellow statice flowers
1 tablespoon of dried orange peel
2 teaspoons of powdered orris root
1 teaspoon of mixed spice
2 or 3 drops of sandalwood oil

Marigold, honeysuckle, mimosa and other lovely flowers combine to make this warm gold and amber pot-pourri. Reserve a few golden rod or yellow statice flowers before you start to scatter on the prepared mixture later. Mix together all the dried ingredients, then add a couple of drops of sandalwood essential oil very carefully. Store in airtight boxes for six weeks.

RED ROYAL

3 cups of crimson rose petals
3 cups of clove carnation petals
1 cup of deep purple pansies
1 cup of rosemary leaves and
lavender flowers
1 tablespoon of ground cloves
1 tablespoon of powdered cinnamon
1 tablespoon of powdered orris root
1 tablespoon of powdered mint leaves
1 tablespoon of powdered bay leaves
3 or 4 drops of rose oil
A few whole rosebuds to scatter over

Rich crimson and purple flowers add depth and excitement to this exotic recipe. Old fashioned rose varieties are particularly suitable as they hold their perfume and colour so well. Place your chosen flowers and herbs into a large bowl and mix gently. If you decide to use the rose oil, add a couple of drops at a time and stir in well. Place in an airtight container for about six weeks, giving the odd shake. Decant into china dishes.

ORIGINAL LAVENDER

~

4 cups of lavender flowers
2 cups of dried thyme
2 cups of lemon mint leaves
½ cup of coarse salt
1 tablespoon of powdered cloves
1 tablespoon of caraway seeds
1 tablespoon of dried lemon peel
3 or 4 drops of lavender oil
Small quantity of blue borage (Borago) flowers

Lavender must be one of the best known and loved of all scents. This simple pot-pourri mixture can be used to fill sachets and linen bags to keep clothes and linen fresh and sweet. Gather your ingredients together, and if some of the leaves appear too large, tear them in half. Place them in a large bowl and mix gently, making sure the salt is combined. Carefully add a few drops of essential lavender oil. Stir again, then pour into air tight containers and store for about six weeks giving the odd shake.

ȘPRING MEMORY

∽

2 cups of red and golden wallflowers
2 cups of mixed daffodils and jonquils
1 cup of mimosa flowers
1 cup of mixed freesia flowers
1 cup of azalea flowers
2 cups of mixed tulip petals
1 cup of lemon thyme
1 cup of variegated pineapple mint
1 teaspoon of dried lemon peel
3 teaspoons of powdered orris root
3 or 4 drops of citronella oil

This lovely pot-pourri incorporates many spring flowers. Its pretty shades and interesting textures will light up a dull corner of your home. Sort through your prepared ingredients, putting by a few whole mimosa and wallflower heads for later. Combine the remainder of the dried flowers, mint, orris root and thyme, mixing them gently in a large bowl. Next add the citronella oil, a few drops at a time. Put the mixture into air tight containers and place in a warm and dry position for six weeks.

$\mathcal{F}$ OREST WALK

∿

3 cups of well dried pine shavings
3 cups small pine cones
2 cups of mixed nuts
1 cup of acorns, very well dried
1 cup of shredded bay leaves
1 cup of cinnamon bark
2 teaspoons of dried orange peel
1 teaspoon of mixed spice
3 teaspoons of orris root powder
1 cup of golden rod or yellow statice
2 or 3 drops of pine oil

This mixture will fill your room with an invigorating fresh pine fragrance. Bowls of this pot-pourri look very effective displayed against a polished wood surface, with a handful of acorns and golden rod or yellow statice on top. Check through your prepared ingredients, discarding any nuts or cones that may show a trace of damp. Mix all the dried items together in a large bowl. Next add two or three drops of the essential pine oil. Mix well, then transfer to dry air tight containers for six weeks.

HARVEST TIME

~

3 cups of crimson rose petals
3 cups of gold and orange rose petals
2 cups of golden rod flowers
1 cup of lemon balm leaves and basil
1 cup of seed heads, wheat or corn
1 cup of peppermint leaves
2 tablespoons of coriander seeds
1 teaspoon of powdered cinnamon
3 teaspoons of orris root powder
2 or 3 drops of sandalwood oil

Harvest shades of crimson, amber and gold combine to make this unusual and attractive pot-pourri. The addition of sandalwood oil leaves a warm lingering woody fragrance.

Place all the dried flowers and seed heads into a large bowl. If using wheat or corn, take off some of the ears, making sure they are perfectly dry. Combine the ingredients ensuring the orris root powder is thoroughly mixed in. Add two or three drops of the essential oil and mix well. Pour into airtight containers for six weeks, then decant.

$\mathcal{A}$UTUMN BREEZE

～

1 cup of bayberry bark
1 cup of buchu leaves
1 cup of small bay leaves
1 cup of eucalyptus leaves
1 cup of pine wood shavings
1 cup of dried seed heads
5 or 6 strips of eucalyptus bark
1 cup of small pine cones
2 tablespoons of coarse salt
1 tablespoon of dried lemon peel
1 tablespoon of mixed spice
6 whole cloves
2 or 3 drops of lemon grass oil

$\mathcal{T}$his masculine recipe has a clean lemon and pine aroma and looks very attractive poured into a simple polished box with a handful of gold helichrysum and cones sprinkled on top. Before you start make sure all the ingredients are completely dry. Mix all the ingredients together in a large bowl. Add the oil sparingly, mix again, and store for six weeks.

*L*AVENDER
BOTTLES

∽

15-20 long stems of fresh lavender
Ribbon or strong string

*L*avender bottles are easy to make and are a pretty and unusual way of keeping clothes fresh and sweet smelling. The method is quite simple but you may need a little practice. Gather together a bunch of long stemmed fresh lavender and tie a thin piece of string or ribbon directly under the lavender heads. Gently bend each stem back separately to encase the lavender heads and make a small cage. Tie another length of ribbon around the stems. Leave a loop of ribbon hanging and allow the lavender to dry naturally before using.

To make a simple and inexpensive gift arrange the lavender bottles in a pretty basket and tie with matching ribbon. Try weaving a length of ribbon through the lavender stems to make the bottle more secure. Pull the ribbon tighter at the top and bottom of the bottle but looser around the centre to ensure an even shape.

$\int$CENTED BAGS

∾

1 cup of strongly scented rose petals
1 cup of lavender
½ cup of lemon verbena leaves
½ cup of crushed rosemary
¼ cup of powdered orris root
2 crushed cinnamon sticks
Few drops essential rose oil

$\mathcal{T}$his simple but deliciously fragrant mixture is perfect for making into sachets and scented bags to place between laundry and bedding. The simplest bag can be made by filling a lace handkerchief with a scoop of potpourri and tying with a piece of ribbon. Pretty bags can also be made from scraps of material you already have. Take a strip of fabric about 19ins (48cms) long by 4ins (10cms) wide. With right sides facing fold the strip in half and sew a narrow seam up both sides. Turn the right way out, fill with pot-pourri, and tie around the neck with ribbon. To make the pot-pourri, mix all the dry ingredients together in a large bowl. Add a few drops of oil until the scent is right. Store in an airtight box for 2 weeks.

$\mathcal{P}$RETTY PARCELS

~

Coloured tissue paper
Gift tags
Dried or fresh flowers to decorate
Pot-pourri mixture (Sweet Rose page 15)
String or ribbon

$\mathcal{A}$ very inexpensive but effective way of gift-wrapping pot-pourri is to place one or more scoopfuls of your favourite mixture onto a piece of triple-thickness coloured tissue paper. Carefully bring the edges up to the middle and tie them with string or pretty coloured ribbon, to make a little bag. Pastel shades of tissue paper look very pretty, especially if you add a matching label or gift tag. For a special effect attach a small cluster of dried flowers, or even a fresh flower to the ribbon or string securing the bag. A small group of multi-coloured parcels placed in a basket or similar container would look delightful for an unusual gift. If you keep a stock of ribbon, gift tags and tissue paper you can create a simple but attractive gift whenever the need arises.